I0517727

Fox Dreams

SAINT JULIAN PRESS
POETRY

OTHER BOOKS BY AUTHOR

Wandering in My Mind

Jack-o-lantern's Adventures in the U.P.

PRAISE FOR FOX DREAMS:

Read *Fox Dreams* and your vision will sharpen page by page, as the speaker's does in "Imagined Darkness," where "a blue jay insists I witness / all the bits and pieces of this life." The exquisite beauty of those bits and pieces lies in the moment in which they are witnessed; an instant of ordinary ecstasy as in "Imagined Darkness": "Your soul is a filament / vibrating inside a bulb..." *Fox Dreams* reveals the partner of beauty as insight. Epiphanies rise like stones in a fast creek. "It is not for me to decide / Every little whim of the sky," the speaker tells us in "In Praise of Porches." "Exhaustion brings the rain / I know that much." Read *Fox Dreams* and intuitional lyricism will free you into knowing, you know more than you thought.

 —Lynn McGee, author of *Tracks, Sober Cooking, Heirloom Bulldog,*
Bonanza, and *Science Says Yes*

Human agency and emotion drift through the marveling world of Laura Smyth's collection of poems, *Fox Dreams*. Birds argue; a woodchuck is surprised; rivers are "less determined," the full moon can "step behind a cloud," irises "search" for what they lack. These poems are portals to the natural world, microscopes and telescopes, invitations to take walks with her along shorelines of seaglass, "bubbling" beneath your feet, to visit the halls of extinction and meet the dodo, and the zoo and consider the escape plans of servals. In a world in which artificial intelligence laps at our feet ever closer and the very fact of existence seems tentative and endangered, Smyth reminds us of swirls of ligaht bending toward us, the presence of both nature and God, the "small bouquets of cold and light and shadow." This is a collection determined to remind us of both the smallest and most sentient details of existence, as well as the brilliant circumstances that make us alive.

 —Elizabeth Cohen, author of *Bird Light,* and
The Patron Saint of Cauliflower

Laura Smyth's fiercely intelligent collection thrums with dreams and visions of the natural world. Creatures of air, land, and water, fields, sunlight, stars, even chemical combustions are revealed by a speaker keenly attuned to Nature and its shadows as well as her own complex humanity. In concise lyrical language Smyth plumbs loss and grief, parenting, danger and safety, aging, regret and other deeply human concerns against a backdrop of the untamed world—the "unscheduled joy" of blue jays, a wind that "turns its body / slowly clockwise / in its own time"—and what we can take from this juxtaposition is at the heart of the collection. Combining a scrupulous awareness of what's often unseen or ignored—a homeless man, a child's drawing, a woman with dementia, servals in a zoo—with an equally unflinching investigation of human nature, Smyth's poems enable us to stop and pay attention, to examine our lives including the distances we maintain and the ones we attempt, and sometimes fail, to cross. Memories and ephemeral moments are captured and held by Smyth's lucid verse as a "bubble is trapped in glass." FOX DREAMS is a clear lens through which we can view our imperfect humanity, both its limitations and the possibilities within.

—Jennifer O'Grady, author of *White*, and
Exclusions & Limitations

Ms. Smyth is an astute observer of nature. And when in this lovely collection of poems she trains her vision on the human soul, the crackling insight always comes, leaving in its wake a satisfying and profound silence.

—Michael Urheber, author of *Bava's Gift: Awakening to the Impossible* and the musical, *The Further Shores of Knowing*

Fox Dreams

poems by Laura Smyth

SAINT JULIAN PRESS
HOUSTON

Published by
SAINT JULIAN PRESS, Inc.
2053 Cortlandt, Suite 200
Houston, Texas 77008

www.saintjulianpress.com

COPYRIGHT © 2024
TWO THOUSAND AND TWENTY-FOUR
©Laura Smyth

Paperback ISBN-13: 978-1-955194-31-0
eBook EPUB ISBN: 978-1-955194-32-7
Library of Congress Control Number: 2024939376

Cover Art Credit: Collage by Smythtype Design
(Public Domain images used from top left "Fox by Mystic Fire," Shibata Zeshin
(1807–1891); hunting fox photo courtesy of the National Park Service; "Fox glove"
New York Public Library Digital Collections; "Dead Fox," Ľudovít Pitthordt,
Slovak National Gallery)
Author Photo Credit: Lily Venable

In loving memory of my mother
Ethel Marie Smyth (Surdam)
for understanding me.

CONTENTS

Fox Dreams

The point must come when nothing matters more
than *who*. *What* has been heard too often; *when*
and *where* renew with shiny bangles stuff
gone dull. It is too late now for *why*.
The question is, "Who is it, is it you?"

—William Bronk,
from "The Extensions of Space," *Life Supports*

Imagined Darkness

Fog to droplets
to raging floods
Inverted, burning hives
of desert ant lions
a blast of solar heat
melts the pavement
as a swift, thin storm
ties itself like a scarf
around the trees' bare shoulders.

Lightning hotter than the sun.
These flashes burn out doubt—
a blue jay insists I witness
all the bits and pieces of this life.

***

Today could be the last
a hummingbird circles past my head

or a chipmunk scatters seeds
across my porch that sparrows later find.

My many clawed neighbors love me without a name
and always return with hunger

and appreciation. If I am still enough
they will gently touch me

that's how I know I'm safe—
because they do not fear me.

***

vindictive against the small
vindictive and distant
claw of night against the stars
one that won't be stilled
one that burns down
all your wishes

***

You know you're wrong
about most things
stories meant to be heroic
are false leads
tragedy is tiny and unseen
until it isn't

***

The moon walks in
and tells you the story
of your life
from a distant speck
neither of you can see clearly
but she's accustomed to reflecting.

***

My girl she always
says no to that imperfect
sham, no shadow
of Platonic forms for her,
a feather duster
shaking up the room.

***

My girl she can always
sense how close
disappointment clings
a perfume
that enters the room before you
powder so fine you can't
help breath it in.

***

Don't come back with trouble
allow the filtered sunlight
to keep traveling through
nothing can stop it, you know
so stop trying.

***

Your soul is a filament
vibrating inside a bulb
containing heat but not light
fracturing, crumbling
igniting sometimes.

***

The sacred eternal domestic
separates
the bone from the flesh
and finds a use for both

saves you from being
either
just the bones
or just the flesh

propels you into a rhythm
even hunger sometimes follows
craving cunning bowing
the sacred eternal domestic
grinds a seed to dust
so it may live again
as bread

I have cried scoured and cursed
so thoroughly
you believe the silent
cleanliness around you
is safe and provided
for you don't
filter too much

dust through your lungs
steady in and out
thickness of air and stock
swimming in love

The eternal sacred domestic
has no reclamation in mind
a wasted infant
is food for someone

and no, the weeping
never ceases
it is the eternal
sacred
domestic

did I not tell you
to put your coat on?
to button up?
to scrape your own plate clean?

I want to be generous
but I have a house to keep
you should
kick the mud off your boots

before you enter
maybe you should crawl
for a time
because fury is also resident

***

Wouldn't you rather just sing?
There are as many birds
as suns—if the sky were endless—
which it is.
So you can be a bird and the sun
afterall. An empty
massive truck goes rattling
down the street
but the feathers swirling
around me are unphased
and go on singing, nesting, squabbling, perching.

Be a sun that is also
a bird.
Have the brightest feathers
you feel comfortable in
but your song
should rumble down any street
you live on
piercing notes above the diesel engines
and crow calls.

***

Crow, my friend at a distance,
flies with a twig
from my backyard to the neighbor's pine tree.
Drinking my bitter coffee
that has gone cold
I sit watching, now in sunlight,
now shadow.

With each cloud we have a different life.

The bones in my body
have told me all about growth
and steadfast love.
As I grow old
and lose patience with the world
they hollow out
like all the shallow places
rabbits nest each summer.

I am young again as I sink in.
Nests of rabbits in my bones.

Driving at Night

If sleep were immediate
I might not notice
time has broken its agreement
to connect one moment with the next.
Shelled in metal
we drive a narrow line through
the windshield's clutter.
A possum crosses at the bend,
red eyes flash and its whole body
arches, unhooks. I turn from him
and am again a child
fallen against the step,
my blood not felt until it is seen.
Rivers are less determined
than that dark stream along my shin.

Servals at the Portland Zoo

They live in a world dressed up,
for children's sake,
to look like the rocks of home,
dark as night through the day
under an electric moon.

How mysterious to feel granite and smell man,
to cross country that never gives way
underfoot or changes face
or has a breeze.

Precision and caution are for prey.
They pace with short, involuntary strides,
absentminded as pedestrians
whose heads are bowed from habit.

When they cross they strike each other
like clumsy boxers. If I strike you
will we know our cage?
We are nervous as creatures certain of escape.

Edie Becomes the Ignis Fatuus

(Ignis Fatuus—foolish fire. A phosphorescent light seen hovering over marshy ground and believed to mislead travelers off their path.)

1.
The horizon is that blank wall
but the sun moves across it
like pictures in a slide show.
An instant. Then another instant.
You dare not blink or half your life
will have lit your face
and you'll be old. And you'll be no more use.

2.
Father always said senility is the mind's way
of counting backwards until it falls asleep.
But I never sleep. I remember
the first moment I left my body.
Here, on the beloved marsh, there is
multiple decay and spawning. Nothing grows
really old. Youth is transformed
into different youth.
You feel the many uses of heat
even in the cool, dark mud.

3.
Blank, dull and drooling
the room contemplates the evening.
I allow the room its scrutiny.
The ticking of nurses. Time
is the pigment on the wall.
Do you remember the first moment
you left your body?
Visitors come and pause,
shadows between vistas.

4.
Forgetting to walk
I gave up feet.
Forgetting children
I left my body by the hearth.
Decades of ridicule and disbelief
haven't stopped this heat.
Self contained. Above the ground.
Don't be afraid of the blank surroundings.
I'm here. You can see by my light.

5.
I am not the grass
or the mud
or the sun.
Not reflection
or what is magnified
A flame doesn't burn itself. It burns.
And I am a flame without even a wick.
The distant light you sometimes catch a glimpse of.
I don't conduct and won't singe,
but skip above the grass, intuitive like joy.

6.
As a girl I'd wake summer mornings
in my attic room, the air heavy, still
with the afternoon heat.
The grass would be steaming, but cool.
So I learned "dew" is not "rain,"
and lightning rises. I used to try
to set the road on fire
but could never ignite the tar.
Mid-day sun and magnifying glass
were only good for paper and skin.
The older, amphibious oils resisted.
Heat, but no flame. A smoldering childhood.
A bright, clear morning
that sees straight through to night.

7.
This sullen darkness like a dream
I never wake from.
Afraid? You can't be
ashamed of yourself here.

I began a glorious life
and then...who was it
set down the lamp
when I became the flame?
Why can't I see out of my own eyes?

One Evening with Erin

One leafless maple at dusk
held to the sky by three fat sparrows.
She is six years old, featherless and unrooted.
She knows how to be the blue air
in the eye of a sparrow
or an exhausted leaf snagged
by the crook of a branch.

She eyes the parentless sparrows
and then explains everything
will die in the next war
as she spins round the tree like the spoke of a wheel.
The air becomes solid. Her body
lives suspended in my mind
and grows old there, finally silenced
by the last thought before sleep.

My niece drew my picture

surrounding me with her
attention, as I am
so far away. Upright

but tilted I'm stuck here
on top an inverted
pyramid—or is it

a kite my body flaps
above? A kite free of
its tether, and me free

of my tether, a flag
of myself? Proportion
has a child's logic. Skimmed

across a yellow sky
I never diminish.
There are triangular

shapes to the body: face
(vaguely), pelvis, a bent
elbow, thumb and finger

extended to the room
or closed holding a pen.
New ideas knit into

her skin after any
injury. What does this
three-cornered-pedestal

mean holding me by my
feet? She's drawn me attached,
a pointer in the hand

of a geometry
lesson. "Today, we'll talk
of powerful desert

architects. What can you
say about proportion?
The geometrical

shape as large as the woman?"
Little girls don't theorize
about their aunts, it would

not be sufficient.
There are beautiful shapes
to intersect before

mathematics interferes.
And besides, she couldn't
set me down all alone,

I'm not that big and there's
all this space
constantly surrounding me.

One Instance

Sun blistered the asphalt.
A stranger spat in my face.
I would have beaten him
if I had a stick.
Heat blistered under trucks and shoes.

The man who spat at me
wore no shoes. I'd have beat him
with my fists. He seemed a mirage
moved by the heat. He didn't expect
my violence, turning on him.

He ran exactly like a dog
flees a cruel master, exactly like
a dog trapped by children
throwing stones from outside a fenced yard.
The heat was not compassion. I am not

master in this yard or any other.
In an instant the day ended.

• • •

It was a bright day
and the man hurried.
He passed so close
his lips nearly brushed my cheek.
For an instant it was like being struck.

I spat anger after him like fat from a fire.
He ran and ran until there were buildings
and whole streets between us.
The asphalt burning
and we two, we touched
and jumped apart in the shock of evaporation.
Don't trust my body:
a neighborhood consumed by fear,
burning and rebuilding,
not wasting any tissue.

Exposure

He wanted a chase.
I heard him start to run
and turned to face him.
The morning traffic passed by unconcerned.
"Don't turn your back on me
I'll kick your ass."
Again and again I must explain
"No, Officer, he did not
have an erection." The law is very specialized,
his gratification is a serious matter.

It's spring,
the ducks are copulating.
The bald hen struggles again
and again to be less favored,
to go unnoticed. Spring,
the ducks will soon be laying.
Each noisy brood will scatter and take mates.
Tonight my neighbor tried again to kill herself.
She couldn't remember what she'd waited for—
a lover? A prudent life?

At the Lily Pond in the Botanic Garden

A woman, bent in the morning light,
already forgets us as she begins
"Please excuse the intrusion, but I'm hungry..."
The history of this moment—one piece of bread
nudged along the surface of the pond
by a feeding turtle: each snap pushing it further away.
My attention wanders between bread and fish and someone's hands.

Deep brown water and tangled roots,
a mass of leaves, half sunken, half lifted,
like snarled hair. Can you prove,
after a certain age, who you are?
Carp, brilliant root among the lilies,
I have mislaid something.
A blackbird cocks its head as though to tell me.

She was unexpected. Stepping back,
I forget again the taste of venison,
whose money I'm spending—
whole stretches gone, as though life is made of sips
then setting down the glass.
A woman cocks her head and speech escapes me.
I wished to give her all my attention.

Flounder

The air is bad and the sun clouded, its bright patches
memory swamped in an aging mind.
"You are a child of God," a fisherman tells me.
The sky blinks down on the boat to remind me.
"You are a child of God,"
I say to the flounder
whose eyes have dried in the sun.

Nights at home I skim the surface of sleep and never settle.
Sometime in the night Mother will drift
with her pillow through the house
looking for a place to rest.
Each night is the same,
for her body has aged into faithlessness,
her skin so sheer it mistrusts everything it touches.

She is a child of God—risen, lured up and sinking.

Laurel Lake

A rower is coming into dock.
My eyes strain through the glare off the water
and catch the face, healthy but strange,
as it shifts forward and back with the oars.
You are everyone I half-see.
Seated at the edge of the lake
my thoughts swell and then blunt against the bank.
Dead, I remind myself. Buried.
Even the bodies I imagine for you
shrivel in this late sun.

My mind is a wasps' nest set on fire.
You are no longer tormented.
I have these flaming thoughts
extinguished by the slapping water.
Waves slip up the bank then turn back
on themselves. So might air
and light and sound
recreate my time with you—the motion
of a bird snatching fish from the lake.
Here, and here, and here.

The Fishing Trip

For Philip Repp, Sr.

1.
The heat is unbearable here
and brings down sweat from the air.
We drape our nets on the water like sheets
on a bed and the small fish
come up thrashing, their scales like polished lead.

There's one bright yellow marsh bird
and two old women fishing eels.
The salt marsh tries to hold us back,
tries to keep the rotting grass,
grass shrimp and shiners.

Our boat stubs into every wave
then slaps down in the hollow after.
I never was a proper fisherman
but they bring me anyway,
my father and my uncle—

the living and the soon dead—
launched onto Great Egg Harbor down the Tuckahoe,
like all the rivers of South Jersey,
smooth and thin as veins
withdrawing from the cold.

2.
We can't talk about this.
I smile at him, smooth within
his smooth hospital sheets,
and he lifts one hand
at the wrist to greet me.
Inside, his body's drowning and soon his mind.
Father sits by the bed, reading.
His face keeps a surprised expression
every day for weeks, his eyebrows
slightly raised and his eyes wide
as if his thoughts were just broken
and he is anxious to answer me.

3.
The deep, deep silence in the hollows
of his skin. I place my hands
to my ears but cannot hear the cells bloom
and collapse or the streams
that feed them. How did his body
prepare for this? A bay
trapped and rolling in his sleep
and our small boat
so trustworthy in the tide.

Morning at Laurel Lake

Turtle wriggles through sunlight
until my shadow falls over the shallow
edge of the lake. The red, sandy bottom
and his glass-like claws I shade
with my curiosity. A dark mind
and a dark, gliding shell.
My shadow is not my intention.
My shadow belongs to the hot day and the sun.

An unbroken mass, memory,
that eventually lightens and breaks loose
like a boat cut from its anchor.
Is that death? A mind reeled in, then unmoored;
an evaporating mist that seems to settle
on the lake while it disperses in air?

I keep trying to understand it,
the death of the body.
I've been jerking toward it
as a school of fish will suddenly turn,
as a hooked fish, not yet landed,
turns and sinks the barb deeper into its mouth.

Turtle holds still and waits for light.
A small school of minnows swerves between us.
Like one finger, bending, they swim under the dock.
I dangle my feet to them
and they nudge me, tasting.
I would stay here forever. I would be the bait
for these small mouths to nibble.
My own hooked ornament, this body.

Non Sequiturs of Comfort

1. Please Wait During the Silence
These years, vibrating wires,
are not connected.
Please wait and the silence will
forget you, your head full
of minerals and multiplications.
Havoc proceeds quietly.
Air globes it.

Body, barbed hook
run through a shadow,
I had to exhaust myself
to look at you. A kernel of age,
random shape my parents made
then named, my prop—
every hair intuitive.

If you wait, silence,
it will not be pleasant.
On my fire escape a robin
creates havoc from spring.
Glass bars it.
Transparent, lucid,
perfect, solid silence.

The fan revolves and heat,
a body that the blades dismember,
is sound as much as feeling.
Monotonous. Visible in sweat.
A humid current in the walls.
Zinc gently vibrates in the bulbs.
Please, the silence will not stop
and inside that age, that calculation,
a bird song or mathematical formula.

It could make sense,
but this electrical breeze
silences thought. Years.
One steamy breath on the window, drying.
That quiet, evaporation.
Then another year exhales.
It could be we've made up our minds
to die silently.

2. Evening News
What inside thought keeps me.
Stopped. Hushed.
Inside what idea
such grief,
alive and frantic,
drowns like an exhausted swimmer.
One absolute moment of helplessness
sums up every other.
Reflective shimmer
then the bottom mud.

On what street could be
such grief. What blank,
gray sky, bird's nest,
torn upholstery, anything
could compel such.
A screen
a flicker and a voice
politely dismembering.
Made of electric current.
Stopped by no real thing.

3. Here
We watch for the dead
faces on every reflective surface.
There are your eyes.
There are anyone's.

One false step remembering.
See what your eyes knew
years ago. No safety,
only remembrance

a useless thing. An instrument
of torture. The incessant
back-beat thumping through the ceiling.
The idea of you.

4. Loop
Flesh draws calcium from the bone
honeycombing sandstone
supporting an empty place,
hollow, resounding space;

If the loop of fever
which returns to my body each spring
dissipates
(an echo
felt in the inner ear—
fear in silence
after so much sound)
my thoughts would condense
from this thin haze which clings like scent.

It is not vastness that frightens me,
but the tiny intimacy
within the body.

5. *Succumb*

If the cold and neutral sea
could please you, could slide the weight
from your skin and leave

the sight in your eyes,
the sensation of breaking
thought on thought,

your mind the grainy beach awash
with all that moves it, never
one thing again, never shown

your one body whole again
but your multitude awash
and glistening

If the sea were my hand
closing your eyes, gently,
for the exhaustion of your body

is so complete,
then the buoyancy of molecules
is remembered as one by one

they succumb and dream
of themselves and their endless families
also washing away from you.

Once, in infancy,

I slept so soundly my lungs forgot me.
If I dreamt, it was snow falling.
Father climbed the treacherous staircase, suddenly glacial,
to find me like a treasure in a snow bank,
and raced down to my mother
screaming "the baby, the baby,"
and Mother called me back as she does my sister
who runs across the forbidden street
chasing the cat, or a toy.

My father might tell it differently
concerned as he was with each step
and how it felt to hold his youngest daughter
dead, he thought forever,
but choking awake
as though this were all ordinary.

Thus I am resurrected
and do not dream of another life.

Phone Call Home

For my father

Pale, almost ghostly yellow,
green of the newest corn stalk,
the blessed foliage flags us on every corner.

The world slips back—
he will not die this way yet—
a slower disease, an older age.

Still I am surprised
by each new shade of green outside my window.
Here is no tragedy, just April in haste

and the grace of almost translucent blue
in my window box. Home, exhausted.
Sunlight just before darkness falls,

two finches argue in the trees,
crocus irregularly dot the hill.
A car passes, a child shouts,

the cat rolls over and sniffs the breeze.
All regret is haste.
Old palms burnt to ashes.

"The people laid branches before him
as he entered the city."
And we are the branches.

Daily

1. Railway Platform
In such light time moves without us.
Vision, on the railway platform, shifts.
Sunlight hangs around us like a mist.
The scattered passengers, exhorted
by the pigeons to move on,
stand trestlelike and stare
with one concerted effort down the track.

One day's beginning.
What slipped between the light
and time but ordinary confusion?
Chipping paint on the trestle transformed to a garment
for the crucified Christ. One tired glance
and god became the tree he died on

and he died again for these commuters.
A starling, small apostle, waddles down the rails
nodding left and right to witness
more than a trick of light
as on the railway platform peace descends.
The pigeons take flight and the notion settles
that human comfort
and human suffering are the same.

2. Without a Sound
They filmed it.
"A man fell to his death..."
as though it were a greeting.
Sunlight, firelight, smoke,
an unnamed man, then the next news item.
One day's conclusion.

I've tried to think cell-by-cell
about death—that constant reconsumption.
Are there misgivings at the level of chemistry?
They were not the blazing petals of a rose he sank to
though we watched him fall, disbelieving,
the burning building collapsing around him.

(to watch a bee crawl up
from deep in a flower
ashen with pollen...)
There was sunlight there also,
and the miracle of time,
but no garden.

A shout, or a shell, or a brief wave of terror
breaks across the room
then sinks into the next commercial image.
I have no idea what became of his body
but that it was broken.

3. Routine
He moves between the standing passengers
pausing only near women.

(The slow motion movement of plants in water:
the rapid, random darting of the fish.)

Nightmares have left our sleep
and here they are, real men, real women.

Where could I go?
No one touches, despite the crowd.

He stands very still as though hiding
among the swaying women.

"I'm safe," he says directly to me.
Then, more softly, "I'm safe."

Sunlight poises on the threshold
afraid to enter here.

4. Crux
The dew is gone by 7 a.m.,
a film of heat already rising from the grass.
Yesterday a cardinal sang from the oak tree.
This morning a goldfinch drops
like a dead weight through the lilac
then flutters back up and out of its branches.

Small birds were loudest hours ago,
now mainly crows shout from the shadiest branches.
Heat mobs my skin and moves me back to the house.
On the news a young man bound and stiff hangs from a tree.
I think for a moment this is fiction.
Then, incredibly, the push in for a closeup of his face.

Close, on his face, nothing his mother can lay claim to.
We are given the screen of his disfigurement;
a horror that moves like light through the heat of the room.
Not the same heat, but the same morning. Everyone will be up soon.
Knives were used a voice is saying.
I see him dead almost as one hears a rumor.

Outside, a surprised woodchuck clambers back into the brambles.
I can smell the tar of the river pilings
and from here see smooth patches
where the current barely moves. How is it
his mother forgave them
when they knew exactly what they did?

"Little we see in nature that is ours…"

1.
Darkness so complete I feel the stars' combustion.
Each point named and important as God, but visible.
Just this moment not in despair.
The lake, the woods and the stars. I thought I understood
my body's longings and my mind's response:
a long, cold silence
breaks into crackling light
as if an old language is reclaimed in conflagration.

If I could believe in anything
it would be this light again
as it crinkles and rebounds off the lake.
Not light itself but what it becomes
on my skin and in my eyes. The finite heat
within my body flares up and has its echo.

2.
Street lamp too bright to show the moon—
step back and let your eyes adjust.
The seamless nature of the optic night
is not the same as this light
flashing safety through exposure.
Out walk it.
Out think your safety
and find the thrum of darkness
when the full moon steps behind a cloud.
An iris opens in search of what it lacks.
The old hooped darkness, uneclipsed.

3.
As though eclipsed in this life by the next,
an old man stares at nothing straight ahead.
"Transfixed" is the poetic term for dead.
He's gone from home because there is no home.
I want to think his mind's gone dark and numb
because that's safer than his mind's aflame.
I accept this and step off the train.
I have no time to think about old men at work.
My computer, left on from the day before,
is solid flickering stars at 9 a.m.
The "Night Sky" saved my screen from burning
one image permanently on its surface.
I cannot place an old man anywhere.

4.
Moonlight spread too thinly over pasture
settles on the horses and the wire fence
between us, barely visible.
The horses startle at a passing car
then step back to the safety of the barn.
The movement of headlights spins us
like tops released from strings
and when the darkness stops us
we are apart. Their skin resettles
with a gentle flapping. I place my will
in the damp grass near them and let it doze.

5.
Damp night air flaps at my screen
heavy as a quilt snapping dry on a line.
Tonight extremity lights our windows from outside.
A storm eclipses sirens;
each clap of thunder reprimands the rumble of this city.
Neighbors talk softly at their windows;
the tone of their privacy rests with the cool air
on my forehead. Clattering supper dishes,
children hurried in to safety from the rain,
the path rain takes along the maple;
panic then beauty amid lightning.
Voices glimpsed like moonlight between clouds.

6.
Bulldozed field after a night of rain.
A patch of weeds and black-eyed Susans
shelters birds who dart out to feed
among the temporary hills.
Yellow/black, red/black flashes
leave no safety in the dirt,
no home hidden however small.
Something larger will be here soon
and larger and larger somethings
eclipse each habitation.
Sequined chaos swarmed the porch light last night.
Blackbirds scatter over a muddy field.

7.

We've worn out the old words and have nothing new.
We mean redemption, remembrance, hope and despair,
but settle for clichés about the stars.
No swirl of light reaches this porch tonight.
A man rummages my trash for bottles.
Children get treats from the Good Humor truck.
Dimmed, we want words less.
Cheapened by talk, the stars seem not for me.
Charts of constellations I once studied
must have been some conjurer's trick—
the hand quicker than the eye.
What do you see?
The distant light or the near one?

(The title is from a line of Wordsworth's poem "The World Is Too Much With Us")

Dodo

(extinct ca. 1683)

Prostrate on the horizon
there is a light,
and we bless its rising
like defeated bullies.
We are insincere again today.
But tonight, when the sun buries itself
in the dirt of our skyline,
I will make another entry
in my catalog of past life.

A Dodo is a laughable thing,
but also dead.
From the living room you call its name
laughing at me unwilling to dismember
the chicken carcass
I am nevertheless willing to eat.
Dodo, Didus Ineptus—
what have we to laugh at?

Glass

Are you afraid you'll be there
for the melt down? You could be
the very pocket of air
needed for the flame to burn.
A bubble in glass.

The froth on a wave. Small wheeze
off a fin or a silent
mouth bubbling beneath your foot
as the sand exhales. Look here
for more than water.

Look here, for the silica
fuses. The furnace and wind
of an old technology.
Agate, chert and flint—stunning
as the cobalt blue

shards of discarded jelly-
fish. Admiring such lenses,
do you covet the ocean?
Glint and crackle like tin foil.
Evaporation.

Window Sill

The universe expanding while we stay small.
The universe expanding while the snow falls
thinner and faster. My cold
white-box room remains indifferent
to the shift of atoms.
Only so many, now farther apart.

Numbers relieve us of thought. Apart
from the nameless, small
idea at the center of atoms
we have no hope. Smashed houses fall
revealing new uncertainties. Snow, indifferent
to the collapse of atoms, melts into salt despite the cold.

The weather stays cold.
Atoms pause for part
of my lifetime (this indifferent
body) then race on. Further out, small
momentums, further over. How quickly night falls.
They hurry me, these atoms,

each with its atomic
spin and bump. An infinite burlesque for the cold
eyes of God. We still believe in fallen
nature, then spring comes. A partial
thaw and crocus burst like small
universes to defy the indifference

of green space. A finite vacuum—different
from a lawn for just this moment. Atoms
are too big to take seriously now. We hope that smaller
and farther off the heat rekindles. Cold
mind to de-particularize
a flower in favor of a universe. Ideas of time and scale fall

open revealing others and others, each falling
as we rush to find the last. Indifferent
wreckage. We set ourselves apart.
Hurry atoms.
This is a cold
spring and we have become very small.

Over my window sill a universe falls silent. Atoms
end and go on ending. Small bouquets of cold
and light and shadow—each part of a different plane of glass.

Descent

Distant, steady lights.
One faint pulsing distinguishes the bay
from the larger expanse.

To our left, other lights
begin their patient circling.
Our loop complete, we bump

down toward a landing,
hollows forming and filling in us
with each new drop.

I spot the main artery
shrouded in gauze-like clouds.
He anticipated this, but not exactly.

The doctor says starvation, finally, not disease.
The descent of his body has taken all my life
but I've only just seen it.

Devotions

1.

It is that almost-summer disquiet—
sudden growth, more vivid than I remember.
The jerky, involuntary movement of branches
as the wind picks up.
There is no language in it,
just this unfurling darkness within me—
the way a summer storm at the end of a hot day
can bring calm.

2.

The air would come to life.
A breath of grass, a skin of darkness snug around us.
Listening in the heat, the house dissolved.
Downstairs, voices softened with us in mind.
We floated on the dark bed as on a pool. All ears
and memory; the voices separate
and inaudible, like church, but glasses clink.

A perfect summer—solemn, griefless.
Adult voices changed from day to night.
They were alive then, like the grass.
A chair scraped from the table, water from the tap.
Playing cards, most likely.
We waited all day to hear them rest.
Each familiar voice a note we could repeat.
A few hours listening
and they filled the room exactly.
Then those voices made a pillow for our heads.

3.
The luxury of half-darkness in a safe place.
Familiar trees dissipate like fog.
Occasional planes rumble overhead,
their lights mixed up with the sharpening stars.
Such disappearances hollow out language.
An inarticulate view, my breath on the glass.
Soon, even my fingers will vanish.
Ice breaks from the railing; smoke drapes the trees.
Finches, who have turned so dark,
come to my window against the cold.
Wind has nothing to say about it,
perched on thin ice, trembling in the branches.

4.
Small eyes under the porch watch for their opportunity.
A spider peeks up between slats
finds nothing small enough and slips back.
A nuthatch pounds its beak up and down a nearby pine,
its breast the reddish-brown of the folded bark.
I'm lulled by a soft cacophony of birdsong and distant traffic.
The fatigue of a long day mocks
the fatigue of long illness. It seems he went to sleep.
We repeat to each other he went to sleep.
And all those speechless hours, barely breathing,
he did not relive regrets.

5.
Window boxes moldering with last year's twigs
hint nothing of spring's upheaval yet.
Pain descending and lifting like a drug
has left me stupid and entranced.
The prodigal doves return to their unsuccessful nest
taking up the burden of my worst fears.
Poor bundle, born on the heels of my bereavement.
You've made my body loved and sorrow full.

6.
This lifetime is cool dusk
slipping down through blades of grass.
I am tired and easily mislaid,
so small in this green forest.
Sometimes it is pleasant to be singular
amid a vast assemblage.
But not always. Not today.

This lifetime pools within me, slowly rippling.
Neighbors' voices drift in snippets
across an acre of sunlight.
What is murky at dusk
is now reflected and I study it,
my chair pulled close
to the edge of the dock.

Unforeseen

A fighter jet juts out over the prow
like a gleaming pine needle pricking the fog
above the cheery "Season's Greetings" stenciled
on the Carrier in New York Harbor.

I credit the accuracy
of their message, delivered here cleanly and silently
as this one gray tonnage sits still amid
a frenzy of water and traffic lights.

It is the surface they had available.

Girl in the American Museum of Natural History

The next case shows how coral
is a bud producing rock, like a mouth
whose teeth are on the outside,
or a body within a bone.
It moves by growing.
The girl keeps her ear pressed to the glass display case,
listening for the clamor
inside each bustling skeleton.
She can see now her own voice
is a polyp and when she shouts
whole new colonies of sound echo back.

Now

Too sparse
I've pared down to almost nothing
but the milk that flows for you
little poem
one breast drips its excess
waiting for you to finish the first
sounds but no words
smile and scratch and cry
I have the scars of you
within my body
and across my body
each new touch like punctuation
too sparse to be discerned
an occasionally dripping faucet
is how my mind works now
small doubts scratched out between bus trips
feeding sessions, feeding perception
from the lip of sleep
not quite an idea growing
but a deep ache like the anticipation
of regret. Perverse this confusion
of joy and panic I find motherhood to be
small body and enveloping mind
another year scratched off
the tiny wreckage of each morning
your bare feet on the grass
confusing the pattern of dew and webs
that moments ago was a fairy land. For you
heaven comes all the way down to the ground
where the shadow of a maple lies on the gravel walk
where each tint of green is an all-over-again

creation like the personable trees, nodding
and sleeping, the sometimes panic
of a breeze, my body a shelter,
my work to see
the last transforming moment of the day.

String Theory

Impossible things like the surface of the earth
but with two more dimensions
a child's toy suspended above a crib
chalk drawings and seabeds
currents, eddies, rocks and piers.

Then the mobile swings
and what becomes of creosote bushes and railroad ties,
row on row of dilapidated fences backed by
swarms of cherry blossoms?
Beauty is more like oxygen than we knew.

Try to imagine any shape to the universe
and a nagging fear rises of
unnumbered houses burning
like the forests they replaced, burning
to a cold, constant pressure at the center.

A child attached but adrift in the mother's body,
a warning buoy,
a lotus before it blooms.

String Theory, II

and what if atoms are not constrained but are adrift
all the yelling children in the yard
the crows in the trees
confirm my suspicions

I have drifted too far afield
I am adrift
drifts of snow are still months off
is that time or space you are describing?

assuring her sleep is not death
has become the nightly ritual
proof is important to a child
the world is entirely in her hands

you can't keep this up forever you know
but she can, seemingly
inexhaustible fear, inexhaustible joy
like day and night

the light and dark ideas of childhood
absolutes so fantastic we don't remember always
our poor cramped minds
come undone and looking to rest

Falter. Forever. River.

1. Canyon Memory
Asphalt giving way to dust and scrub pines,
a canyon explored for the first time
on my bike with ten years of life
riding into so much sunshine, alone, but still tethered.

I don't remember a single sound
only the rise and fall into shades of brown,
chasing whatever speed I could
in the warm enclosure of the mountains.

2. Forever
So late, and I'm still
considering sleep wide awake.
It is never absolutely quiet here.
Or dark.

A fan hums in the next room
like a distant river.
Thoughts drown in that sound
but sleep still falters.

As though no time has passed,
or forever has passed,
Father sits at the kitchen table shuffling cards.
I did not intend

to still be grieving this way.
A dry river bed.
A sleepless night.
The kitchen has not been put in order yet

and now the simple act of rinsing a glass
can raise the dead. Snap of the deck
as an old man, younger again,
makes his continued, momentary appearance,

steps into the current of my darkened house
and is swept along with masked thoughts
and sleeping intentions
like well-worn stones.

3. *Still*
Bird song, cigarette ash and oak leaves
large and small ants burdened with debris
the leaf that looks like a bird that becomes a bird—
the only still thing on the branch.

Early evening July light, a persistent joy,
the voices of crows and children,
rustling trees and distant hammering,
the rising hum of locust broken here and there by a passing car.

A starling chatters, absentmindedly picking through the grass.
Buoyancy and stillness—the children twirl,
kick and tumble in the water—
Watch this, they call, *watch this.*

Winter Driving

Four white-tailed deer bolt
As the low flame of sunset ignites the orchard.

Directly, we fall silent, lacking conjunctions,
broken hearted. Hooves and a dusting of snow,

muffled pounding. It always comes back to that
black hole at the center—neither matter nor half-moon—

flames of ice pierced by headlights.
Without fear of gravity

momentum will get you over the next rise
or into the soft, dark shoulder.

Even small failures are unforgiven.
The one thing you may never do is stop.

Deer leap in four directions over drifts
that go black outside the range of our beams.

Broken hearted or not, a doe stands in the pelting storm
just taking it.

Home, Suddenly

Standing between houses, half home,
partially lit by stars and snow's rebounding light.
My daughter peers from the window as snow drifts
against the cedar hedge sheltering the rabbits.

Standing between lives
snow spreads before me like a crumpled page.
Never such a blank sheet to fill.
A rabbit plays dead in the snow

cunning, faux-frozen, then gone and
I'm left staring at all the gaps I have created,
risks not thought about in years—
my daughter's face backlit in the kitchen window.

Crows in Copper Harbor

Pouncing like feathered cats across the grass
these crows are fussy and determined scavengers,

their scolding voices clear the yard
of any smaller birds and also me.

Back inside I fight the urge to flee.
My window frames the willows red-tinged leaves.

I'm not sure I want to know what these birds teach.
Inside my wooden walls I watch the trees.

Fault Line

Daylight moon over my shoulder.
Cool smooth boulders under my feet.
Wave after wave collapses on the beach.

I am standing on the fault line—
a million lifetimes folded, pressed,
and washing away to gravel without complaint.

Water's steady conversation with the shore
ends here attended by loved ones
who do not know us yet.

What the Wind Is

memory thrown clear
cold teeth at the back of your neck
the beating no one deserves
pinned down then tossed aside
space without peace
and the speed of the universe
passing us by

Listen

Birds voices all through the trees,
my neighbors hammering at their houses
make a percussive accompaniment to this morning's music.
I'm happy to sit and hear them all
even the young man in the red truck
who floors it through the midline of town
seeking...something his soul craves (I think)
but more likely late for work.

Listening, always listening.
I wish I could join them,
my neighbors,
the birds.

Walking By Lake Superior With My Daughter

Eagles focus twice—
overlapping circles pinpoint shade
below the water's surface.

We're rooted in their shade,
left to scavenge through feathers or strain our focus
on the hope of an updraft. "Tears,"

I think—"rafts of tears"—
but that's just hyperbole.
I try to keep my focus

away from the carnage being done to a doe's carcass
on the sand. My daughter reaches
back to draw me up, scavenging

through years, shading
my memories with her own. Look, or look away—
I may as well argue with a shadow

on the beach. This morning we focus
on breathing, as the wind pierces our lungs.
Shade of wings, then clouds, whip past. I could reach her

if she'd please not tear at me.
More than broad wings, it takes heat to soar
and hollow bones.

I've watched her tear fruitlessly for years.
Her focus centers on the eagle overhead—
it's shadow obscuring the feast—

that mother's body—
as more birds land and tear
into her sustaining shade.

Fox Dreams

The smallest hearts
linked and branched
with the strongest wishes.

Here is a cat and a breeze
and aching, burning feet
but nothing stays long,

nothing really has to last in June. We can wait
for August. Quail, ruffed grouse
robins' eggs in the birch branches.

What nest withstands
what wind? What branch
cracks with tonight's storm?

Three crows in the willows
have had enough sorrow
and are impatient with me

dawdling here as though I don't know
what is expected from a carcass.
No rational scavenger picks daintily.

The crows glide off—
one dark arrow against the robin's-egg sky—
My leading edge of joy.

Grow like a leaf,
swell like the wind.
So many sounds fill this morning

and all I want to do is watch the trees.
A swaying branch casts its inverted image
on the grass where the crows now lounge.

The wind returns early and with such grace
ruffling feathers on the lawn
nudging a dragon fly resting on a patch of stones

then turns its body
slowly clockwise
in its own time.

Blue Jays

Blue, unscheduled joy flocks to the cedar hedge
flashing stained-glass wings and
mocking the house-bound cat.
Evening primrose sweetens the breeze.
All wildflowers bloom at once
in this rangy, lanky, summer
that tramples the scheduled joys of August.

Branches downed from the birches
are peaceful relics of last night's storm
as the sunset tugs the lake up to the sky.
All is swept to a vanishing point—
another day reduced to a dark whisper—
where it is so clear even the dew
is alive and hopeful.

Girls' Dress Code

Mourning doves land in the pines
their twig-like legs camouflaged
by branches overhung with snow.

Landing and flying, old memories
settle like bread on the crusted ground—
A mile to school and back with legs sacrificed to sleet.

My daughter can't imagine such a silly thing
as mothers slipping pants on under skirts.
Here where cold is our sacrament

I think I'll write "It does not matter!"
ten thousand times in the snow
because we never called it what it was.

Elsewhere

The cracked pavement was lined with ice
and every few blocks a woman begging.
"Jesus loves you...children, I was so sick...if you could just help
  me...."

One face mocked, another deeply concentrating.
Voices snapped like branches laden with ice.
Bracketed life, I think, here is the mistake, there the deletion.

Now bombs fall on kitchen tables and children's beds
while I sit, coffee steaming between my hands,
and the snowfall relentlessly furthers the hush.

I continue my battle with the cold. Hidden in my sleep
are the nests of fallen children and forgotten rooms.
But I am always too late. Always.

It could be the year 1964 or the year one.
A small girl sits on a patch of dirt
looks up and brushes the dust from her hands.

Love is degrees from freezing.
Because children are burning
we will wake up tomorrow to the same flames.

The veneer of numbers

flattens me again,
particles of something then nothing
left to circumnavigate the globe.
Two dimensions can't quantify
greater or lesser sorrow:
Love me because I do not measure
but slip on stray thoughts
flung across the beach, over the lake,
into the wings of geese and herons,
shaken loose in time

A flock of simple failures

wanting to take flight
we stay tethered long enough
for gravity to catch up

the pain of separation
relieved by repetition
generation after generation

linear as a root
seeking water
salt that finds the wound

delicate—harboring—
I almost saw it—
turned—and nothing past

wandering nightly
as though every door ever closed
must be reopened

I remember seeing from the back seat
the whole nation
and what seemed like endless sunlight

I Will Never See the Rio Grande

From the morning I salvage the shadow of a hummingbird
and later the evening light
running off from the west facing cherry tree
hurrying the chipmunks
to gather more.
Never enough.
Children are playing under the trees
their voices as vibrant as the crows.
I am relieved to hear them
not drowning
in a river in Texas
but then I remember where I am
and how to listen
to children playing in order
to salvage something lovely from the day.

I do not live near a river
of fearful people.
Not now. Perhaps
my day in the river
is coming. Tonight
robins are singing back and forth
about the fading summer—
no that's my song.
I have not even one acre
but in this space I salvage
everything in the world
which comes to me.
It is not enough.
It is so small
the weight of it
pins me to my chair.

In Praise of Porches

It is not for me to decide
Every little whim of the sky.
Exhaustion brings the rain
I know that much.

I used to think the wind had one voice.
Like Chopin shouting—"The world hurts—pay attention..."
Or perhaps Bach proclaiming—"The world is beautiful—listen..."
But it's not for me to decide

What notes the newly-fledged sparrow shares with the sun.
She feasts while I fade away.
I pace between two heavens
Both shabby and covered in greens.

One faces east, the other west
And because they have been long-loved
They stoop a little
But the sun is just as strong.

Daylilies by the birch trees
Open with the colors of sunrise
And listen with me
to the sparrows.

Acknowledgments

All the poems in this book have been improved by the careful reading and genuine feedback of many writers and friends over the years. I am deeply grateful. But the limited space, and the narrow constraints, of acknowledgements have sent me back to my beginnings to call out special acknowledgement for three poets whose work I admire and whose teaching made it possible for me to imagine myself as a poet.

First, Primus St. John, whose writing workshops at Portland State University (where I was an opinionated undergrad) started me on this path.

Second, Sandra McPherson, who taught me, among many other things, that no one can tell you if what you've written is a poem except yourself. Write what you want to write.

And third, Richard Hugo, whose one-week workshop on the Oregon coast a few years before his death lifted my confidence regarding what work I should be doing and potentially could be doing.

Publication Credits:

"Laurel Lake" published in *The Southern Poetry Review* (1988)

"Edie Becomes the Ignis Fatuus" and "The Fishing Trip" published in
	The Denny Poems 1989–90

"Non Sequiturs of Comfort" published in *1990 Quarterly*

"Phone Call Home" published in *Metiphors.* (1997)

"Railway Platform" published in *The Light In Ordinary Things*
	(Fearless Poetry Series, Fearless Books, 2009)

"Falter. Forever. River." published in *Tiferet: A Journal of Spiritual
	Literature,* Issue 19 (2011)

"Winter Driving" published by Issue 21, Damselfly Press

"Exposure" and "At the Lily Pond In the Botanic Garden", *JJournal,* 2013

"Girl In the American Museum of Natural History" *A Ritual to Read
	Together: Poems in Conversation with William Stafford* published by
	Woodley Press, Fall of 2013.

"Now," "Devotions," "Morning at Laurel Lake," and "Home Suddenly"
	published in *Red Truck Review,* January, 2015

The following poems were also published in chapbook form by Finishing
	Line Press in 2015 under the title *Wandering In My Mind*:
	"Wandering In My Mind," "At the Lily Pond in the Botanic Garden,"
	"One Evening With Erin," "Exposure," "One Instance," "Non
	Sequiturs of Comfort," "Daily," "Servals at the Portland Zoo," "Little
	We See In Nature That Is Ours," "String Theory," "String Theory II,"
	"Glass," "Window Sill," and "Winter Driving."

Sections of the poem "Imagined Darkness" were produced as broadsides for
the Finlandia University Faculty Art Exhibition in Spring 2023.

ABOUT THE AUTHOR: Laura Smyth is a writer, teacher, and book designer (smythtypedesign.com). She holds an MFA degree from Columbia University and spent many years living and working in the New York metropolitan area before moving to the Keweenaw Peninsula of Upper Michigan. Her poetry, which has been published in print and online journals as well as anthologies, is inspired most by the intersection of human nature and the natural world.

www.ingramcontent.com/pod-product-compliance
Lightning Source LLC
Chambersburg PA
CBHW031447120626
46545CB00006B/2599